SEP 2014

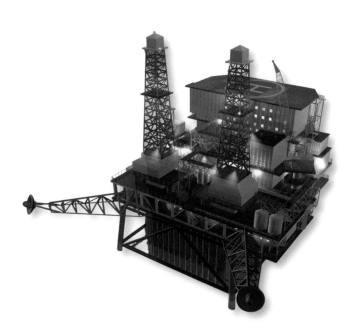

Published in 2014 by The Rosen Publishing Group, Inc.
29 East 21st Street, New York, NY 10010

Credits and acknowledgments
KEY tl=top left; tc=top center; tr=top right; c=center; cr=center right; b=bottom; bl=bottom left; bc=bottom center; br=bottom right; bg=background

CBT = Corbis; GI = Getty Images; iS = istockphoto.com; N = NASA; SH = Shutterstock; TPL = photolibrary.com; wiki = Wikipedia

front cover CBT; bg SH; **4–5**c TPL; **6–7**bg iS; **7**tc, tr iS; **9**c GI; **11**b TPL; **12**br GI; bl iS; **13**bl, br CBT; **14**bc iS; **18**tr SH; **20**tr N; **20–21**b iS; **21**tr CBT; tl GI; cr iS; **22**bc iS; **24**bc iS; **26–27**c GI; **28**bl CBT; tr iS; br SH; **28–29**bg iS; **29**br iS; tr SH; bl, tl wiki; **30**bg, br, tr iS; tc N; **32**bg iS

All illustrations copyright Weldon Owen Pty Ltd. **25**c Andrew Davies/Creative Communication

Weldon Owen Pty Ltd
Managing Director: Kay Scarlett
Creative Director: Sue Burk
Publisher: Helen Bateman
Senior Vice President, International Sales: Stuart Laurence
Vice President Sales North America: Ellen Towell
Administration Manager, International Sales: Kristine Ravn

Library of Congress Cataloging-in-Publication Data

Einspruch, Andrew, author.
  What is energy? / by Andrew Einspruch.
    pages cm. — (Discovery education. How it works)
  Includes index.
  ISBN 978-1-4777-6321-6 (library) — ISBN 978-1-4777-6322-3 (pbk.) —
ISBN 978-1-4777-6323-0 (6-pack)
  1. Power resources—Juvenile literature. 2. Energy policy—Juvenile literature. I. Title.
TJ163.23.E36 2014
333.79—dc23
                            2013023586

Manufactured in the United States of America

CPSIA Compliance Information: Batch #W14PK2: For Further Information contact Rosen Publishing, New York, New York at 1-800-237-9932

HOW IT WORKS

WHAT IS ENERGY?

ANDREW EINSPRUCH

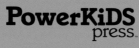

New York

Contents

Energy Sources

Nature provides many forms of energy that people use every day in many ways. Energy powers our homes and vehicles, heats our water, and helps us do our work. There are two kinds of energy sources: renewable and non-renewable. Renewable sources, such as energy from the wind, Sun, and sea, are replenished by nature when they are used. Non-renewable sources, such as oil, gas, and coal, are not naturally replenished as fast as we use them. Once they are used, they are gone for thousands of years.

Where energy comes from

Fossil fuels, such as coal, petroleum (oil), and natural gas, are taken from the ground. Energy also comes from the Sun, and the movement of water and wind.

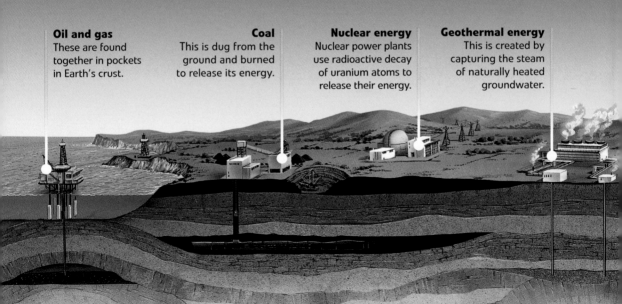

Oil and gas
These are found together in pockets in Earth's crust.

Coal
This is dug from the ground and burned to release its energy.

Nuclear energy
Nuclear power plants use radioactive decay of uranium atoms to release their energy.

Geothermal energy
This is created by capturing the steam of naturally heated groundwater.

VITAL ENERGY

Just as machines need energy to work, our bodies need energy to survive. Everything our bodies do, from thinking to moving, requires energy. We take in fuel when we eat food, then convert that fuel to energy so we can do things. Power describes how fast energy is used.

Running
The amount of energy we burn when running depends on how big we are and how fast we are going.

Food
Foods, such as fruits, are full of fuel that our bodies naturally convert to energy during digestion.

Main sources
Currently, most of the world's energy needs are met using non-renewable fossil fuels, such as coal, oil, and natural gas.

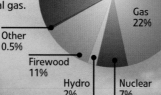

Oil 33%
Coal 24.5%
Gas 22%
Other 0.5%
Firewood 11%
Hydro 2%
Nuclear 7%

Users of energy
Some countries use much more energy than others. The US uses almost 25 percent of the world's energy.

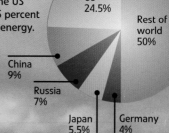

US 24.5%
Rest of world 50%
China 9%
Russia 7%
Japan 5.5%
Germany 4%

Hydroelectric energy
Flowing water turns large turbines to generate electricity.

Wind energy
The force of wind is used to turn turbines and produce electricity.

Solar energy
The Sun's energy is captured and converted into electricity.

Tidal energy
The power of the sea's tides is captured to drive turbines.

Oil and Gas

The world's demand for the energy from oil and gas is endless. However, the supply of them is certainly limited. It takes millions of years for them to form, so creating new supplies is not an option. The hunt for new sources goes on constantly, while known sources are being used up. Getting the best use of these limited resources becomes more important every day.

Oil rig
An offshore oil rig is a huge platform in the ocean. Made from steel and concrete, hundreds of people work there to get oil and gas from below the seafloor.

Fossil fuel reserves
Fossil fuels are found only in certain places, mainly in Middle Eastern countries. These countries sell those resources to the rest of the world.

Natural gas reserves

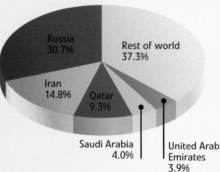

Russia 30.7%
Rest of world 37.3%
Iran 14.8%
Qatar 9.3%
Saudi Arabia 4.0%
United Arab Emirates 3.9%

Oil reserves

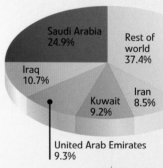

Saudi Arabia 24.9%
Rest of world 37.4%
Iraq 10.7%
Kuwait 9.2%
Iran 8.5%
United Arab Emirates 9.3%

HOW THEY FORM

Oil and gas are called fossil fuels because they form from the fossilized remains of ancient plants and animals, crushed for millions of years by rock.

Falling to the floor
Dead microscopic organisms fall to the floor of the ocean, and are covered by mud and silt.

Building layers
Over time, layers of rock build up. The pressure of these layers converts the organic remains into oil and gas.

Rising up
Where it can, the oil and gas rise through porous layers of rock. However, they are trapped by non-porous layers.

Drilling reservoirs
Where rock layers are just right, oil and gas collect in reservoirs. They are extracted by drilling into the reservoirs.

Risk and reward
Drilling for oil and natural gas is risky, dirty, and expensive work. For the companies that do it, the rewards can be huge because they can then sell these valuable substances.

Coal

Coal formed from the remains of ancient swamp plants that decayed in mud and were compressed by layers of Earth. The pressure of these layers converted the decayed plants into different kinds of coal. Today, we dig this up and burn it to create heat and electricity. Coal is used more than any other energy source on the planet today.

- Rest of world 30.2%
- US 25.4%
- Russia 15.9%
- Australia 8.3%
- India 8.6%
- China 11.6%

Coal reserves
Coal is only found in certain places on Earth. More than two thirds of all coal is found in just five countries: the US, Russia, China, India, and Australia.

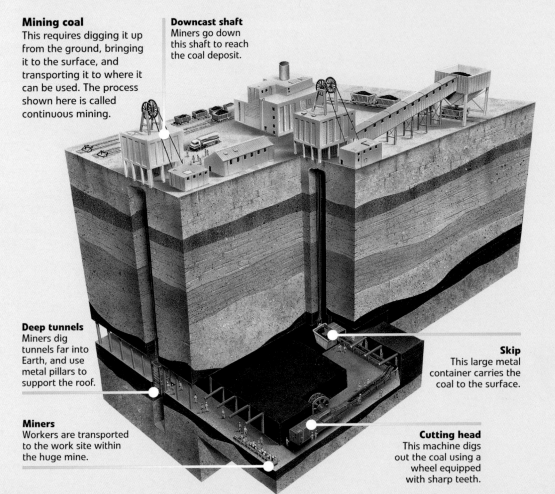

Mining coal
This requires digging it up from the ground, bringing it to the surface, and transporting it to where it can be used. The process shown here is called continuous mining.

Downcast shaft
Miners go down this shaft to reach the coal deposit.

Deep tunnels
Miners dig tunnels far into Earth, and use metal pillars to support the roof.

Miners
Workers are transported to the work site within the huge mine.

Skip
This large metal container carries the coal to the surface.

Cutting head
This machine digs out the coal using a wheel equipped with sharp teeth.

HOW COAL IS FORMED

It takes thousands of years for buried plant material to turn into coal. When this buried material is compressed, it loses most of its water, oxygen, and other gases. The carbon that is left is eventually squeezed into different kinds of coal.

Peat
Decayed plants turn into peat.

Lignite
Peat compressed by rock turns into lignite, or brown coal.

Bituminous coal
More pressure and time turns lignite into black coal.

Anthracite
The best coal, called anthracite, is the most compressed.

Open cut mine
An open cut mine is a huge pit cut into the ground. Materials, such as coal, are then scooped out and taken elsewhere, leaving a huge hole.

Nuclear Energy

Consumer's home

S ome think nuclear energy is the solution to the world's energy problems. Others think it is a dangerous process that leaves behind dangerous materials and should not be used. It is a very controversial energy source. Nuclear energy is created by causing certain atoms, mainly uranium, to react in such a way as to release their energy. This energy is used to heat water into steam, which, in turn, rotates turbines to create electricity.

Making nuclear energy

Small amounts of nuclear fuel react, and the resulting heat is transferred to water. This turns into steam that spins turbines. These, in turn, produce electricity, which is transported by transmission wires to homes and businesses.

Nuclear power station
In 2009, approximately 14 percent of all of the world's electricity was produced by nuclear power stations.

Bombing of Hiroshima
On August 6, 1945, the destructive power of nuclear energy was seen when an atomic bomb was dropped on the city of Hiroshima, Japan.

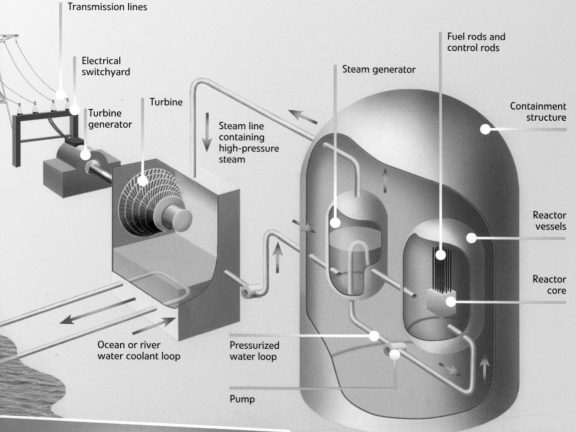

Transmission lines

Electrical switchyard

Turbine generator

Turbine

Steam line containing high-pressure steam

Steam generator

Fuel rods and control rods

Containment structure

Reactor vessels

Reactor core

Ocean or river water coolant loop

Pressurized water loop

Pump

Nuclear devastation
As well as killing 80,000 people instantly, the bombing of Hiroshima flattened most of the city, and left a legacy of radiation poisoning. The eventual death toll was 140,000.

MARIE CURIE

Working with her husband Pierre, Marie Curie discovered uranium and identified how it is naturally radioactive. At her Radium Institute, she studied how it could be used for medical purposes.

Marie Curie worked with uranium, thorium, and other radioactive materials.

Geothermal Energy

Geothermal energy draws on the heat found inside Earth's crust. In some places, steam naturally escapes from Earth. In other places, water is pumped down, allowed to heat, then captured when it comes back up. In either case, a geothermal power plant can capture the steam, then run it through a turbine to generate electricity that can be transmitted to homes and businesses.

That's Amazing!

For every 328 feet (100 m) you go into the ground, the temperature rises by 5.4°F (3°C). So, 2.5 miles (4 km) below the surface, the temperature reaches 250°F (120°C).

Yellowstone hot springs
The hot springs at Yellowstone National Park are a wonderful example of heat in the Earth's crust producing hot water and steam.

Geothermal power station

Cold water is pumped into holes drilled very deep. The cold water is heated by the naturally hot rock below. Hot water resurfaces, where it is used to create electricity.

1 Distribution grid

2 Transformer

3 Generator

4 Turbine

5 Power station loop

6 Heat exchanger

7 Production loop

8 Each mark represents 0.6 miles (1 km).

9 Insulating sedimentary rock

10 Cold water is pumped underground.

11 Water flows through hot, fractured rock.

12 Permeable zone of hot, dry, and fractured granite

13 Superheated water returns to the surface using wells.

Tidal and Hydroelectric Energy

t is possible to generate energy using water. One way is to harness the natural movement of the ocean's tides. Another way is to store water, typically in a reservoir, then direct a flow of the stored water to generate energy. This is called hydroelectric energy. In both cases, the movement of water turns turbines to create electricity. This energy is renewable, so long as there is a source of water.

Did You Know?

The use of hydroelectric energy dates back to 1882. That was when the first hydroelectric station opened in Wisconsin using the waters of the Fox River.

Ebb and flow

Tidal power plants draw on the back and forth movement of tides. Moving water turns the rotors in turbines, which, in turn, generate electricity.

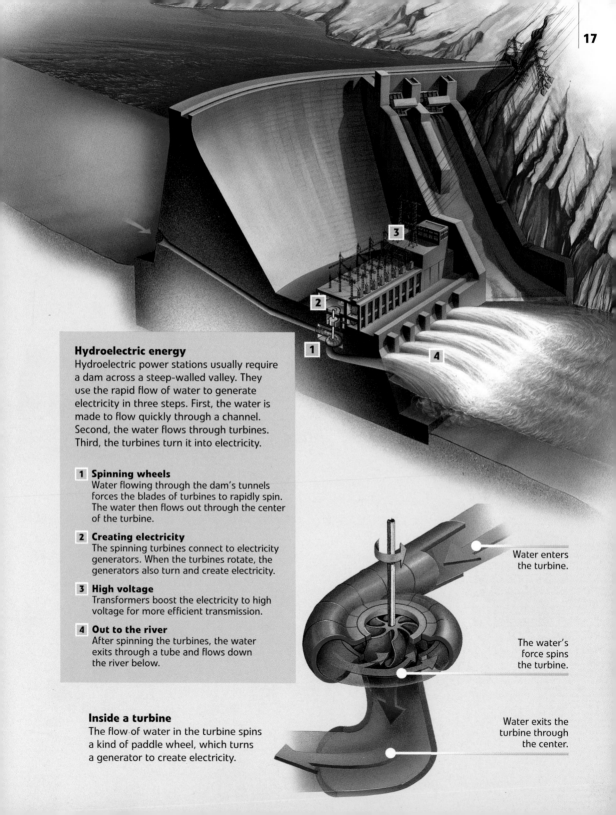

Hydroelectric energy

Hydroelectric power stations usually require a dam across a steep-walled valley. They use the rapid flow of water to generate electricity in three steps. First, the water is made to flow quickly through a channel. Second, the water flows through turbines. Third, the turbines turn it into electricity.

1 Spinning wheels
Water flowing through the dam's tunnels forces the blades of turbines to rapidly spin. The water then flows out through the center of the turbine.

2 Creating electricity
The spinning turbines connect to electricity generators. When the turbines rotate, the generators also turn and create electricity.

3 High voltage
Transformers boost the electricity to high voltage for more efficient transmission.

4 Out to the river
After spinning the turbines, the water exits through a tube and flows down the river below.

Inside a turbine

The flow of water in the turbine spins a kind of paddle wheel, which turns a generator to create electricity.

Water enters the turbine.

The water's force spins the turbine.

Water exits the turbine through the center.

Wind Energy

Wind farms
At the start of 2010, the top two countries for generating wind energy were the US and Germany.

Watch the movement of branches in a tree and it is easy to see that wind has energy. People have long harnessed this energy to help them sail ships and pump water. The modern way to harness the wind is through wind farms, which use giant blades to capture the movement of air and turn it into electricity. Wind energy is clean and renewable and is becoming an increasingly important contributor to the world's energy total.

The very first wind farm was built in New Hampshire, in 1980.

THE WINDMILL

Windmills have been used for more than 1,500 years. The first ones were in Persia (now Iran), and had horizontal cloth sails. These were improved by Europeans, who mounted the sails vertically to catch more wind.

| AD **500** | **1400** | **1850** | **2000** |
| Persian windmill | European tower windmill | Windmill pump for agriculture | Modern wind turbine |

Harnessing the wind

Wind farms must be located in places known to have lots of wind. Computers detect current wind direction and turn the large blades to face it. The spinning motion of the blades is converted to electricity.

Blades
The angle of the blades can be changed to control the response to high winds.

Gearbox
The gearbox is driven by the turbine shaft and controls the generator's speed.

Turbine shaft
The blades turn the central turbine shaft. The speed depends on how much wind blows.

Generator
This takes the spinning motion and converts it into electricity.

Nacelle
This contains the machinery. It pivots to keep the blades pointing toward the wind.

Tower
The blades are mounted a safe distance from the ground on a tower. The tower contains cables that transport electricity to ground level.

Cables
Underground cables collect the wind farm's electricity.

Solar Energy

The Sun releases a massive amount of energy every moment. This energy radiates out from the Sun, warming Earth and supporting all of the planet's life. Increasingly, people are capturing part of that energy and using it to generate electricity and heat water. Many solar systems are installed on individual houses, and it is increasingly common to see solar electricity panels and solar hot water systems on homes. Electric companies are also building more solar panel farms for commercial power generation.

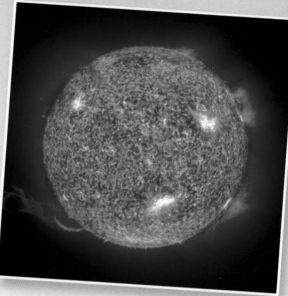

Powerhouse
The Sun has been radiating energy, much as it does now, for more than a billion years. And it will continue to do so for billions of years to come.

Enough solar energy reaches Earth to meet all our energy needs. The trick is capturing it.

Solar panel farms
One form of commercial solar power generation is solar panel farms. These capture the Sun's rays, convert them into electricity, and feed it into the power grid.

TRANSFORMING SUNLIGHT

Solar cells capture sunlight using silicon crystals. The light knocks loose electric charges in the crystals, which are channeled into wires as electrical current.

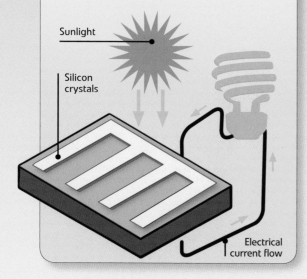

Sunlight

Silicon crystals

Electrical current flow

Cars of the future

Solar-powered cars are still at the experimental stage. But each year, since 1985, solar car races have been held using fully solar-powered cars.

Outdoor lighting

Solar power does not have to be large or fancy. The common solar garden lamp charges during the day, then provides outdoor lighting at night.

Energy from Garbage

A n ongoing problem is what to do with all the trash people throw away. We know we should reduce, reuse, and recycle, but, inevitably, tons (t) of waste ends up buried in landfills each year. One way to tap into this buried resource is to use it as an energy source. A bioreactor located on a landfill can capture methane gas that the landfill creates and use it to make electricity.

WHAT IS IN A LANDFILL?

Up to 90 percent of the trash that ends up in a landfill could be recycled, reused, or composted, and become of value to someone again. The chart below shows the different kinds of waste found in the landfill of a typical developed country.

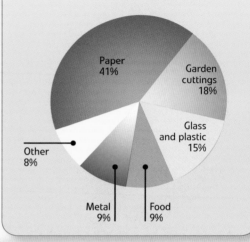

Paper 41%

Garden cuttings 18%

Glass and plastic 15%

Other 8%

Metal 9%

Food 9%

Processing landfill trash
Bulldozers are used to crush and compress waste at a landfill site. This makes it hard for bacteria to decompose the organic matter.

Bioreactors

Machines that use waste as a fuel source are called bioreactors. They capture methane gas released by rotting waste in landfills and burn it to produce electricity. Methane is a greenhouse gas, and using it to produce energy decreases the amount of it that goes into the atmosphere.

Generator
The generator takes the methane and turns it into electrical power.

Energy
Transmission lines transport the electricity to where it can be used.

Liquid
Liquids produced by rotting waste are circulated, which helps the waste break down faster.

Did You Know?
About 60 percent of methane gas comes from human-created sources, such as landfills. The rest comes from natural sources.

Methane
The methane is collected in pipes, which carry it to the generator.

Buried waste
Rotting waste buried in the ground produces methane.

Biofuels

A source of renewable energy that holds tremendous potential is biofuel. This comes from living materials, such as plant waste, crops such as soybeans and corn, and even certain kinds of algae. Most often, biofuels are used to power vehicles as an alternative or additive to petroleum fuels, such as gasoline and diesel. While they have many advantages, such as being renewable and less polluting, biofuels also have disadvantages. It can take a huge amount of energy to produce them, and they can divert farming efforts from feeding people.

PROS	CONS
Based on plants, so they are renewable.	Plants grown for fuel can mean fewer plants grown for food.
Are less polluting than burning petroleum products for fuel.	It can take more energy to produce them than the energy they provide.
Do not contribute to global warming as much as petroleum fuels.	Often impractical to replace more than a small amount of fuel usage with them.
Some, like biodiesel, can be used with little change to existing equipment.	Loss of animal habitats if additional land is devoted to growing biofuels.
Can be made from material, such as grease, that would otherwise become waste.	Can cause other environmental problems.

Ethanol
One kind of biofuel that can be used to power cars is ethanol. Often made from corn, it is mixed in varying percentages with gasoline.

Biofuels in the making

Biofuels harness natural processes in nature. Plants capture sunlight and carbon dioxide. The plants are broken down into sugars, and these are converted into fuel.

Sunlight and carbon dioxide occur naturally in the air.

Plants capture the Sun's energy and carbon dioxide.

Carbon dioxide is reabsorbed by original crops.

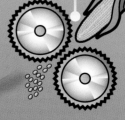

Plants are harvested.

Vehicles release carbon dioxide when fuel is burned.

Ethanol is used as fuel.

Microbes convert sugar into fuel.

Enzymes convert plant material into sugars.

Plant material is processed into small pieces.

Energy-Efficient Home

An important part of curbing the hunger for energy is making homes energy efficient. Around one third of the greenhouse gases produced comes from our homes, so making them energy efficient is not only a great way to save money in the long run, but is good for the planet, too. The good news is that existing homes can be made more energy efficient with only a little extra time and money.

Recycling
Recycling means that new things do not need to be produced from scratch, which takes less energy.

Greenhouse
Sunlight hitting the greenhouse helps to heat the home during cold months. It can also heat water for an underfloor pipe system, which also warms the house.

Composting
Kitchen food scraps and yard clippings can be composted to decrease waste and provide nutrition for the garden.

Insulation and windows
Insulation in the walls and ceiling help to keep heat in during winter and heat out during summer. Double-glazed windows also prevent heat from leaking out of the house.

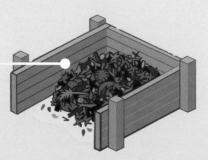

Power
Solar panels and a wind turbine on the roof both contribute electricity to run the home's appliances and electrical equipment. Extra energy is contributed to the local power grid.

Lighting
Skylights and sun-tubes provide natural lighting that does not require energy to brighten a room. Energy-efficient lightbulbs burn less fuel when used.

Hot water
Solar power uses the Sun's energy to provide hot water, decreasing the amount of electricity or natural gas needed.

Appliances
Kitchen and laundry appliances range widely when it comes to how much energy they use. Choosing an energy-efficient refrigerator, freezer, dishwasher, washing machine, and dryer means less fuel is needed.

Flooring
Water heated in the greenhouse circulates through the flooring, helping to keep the house warm. Because heat rises, warming the floor helps to warm the whole house.

Fact File

The world of energy is a fascinating one. There are so many different energy sources, renewable and non-renewable, and so many ways to use them. Researchers are constantly looking for new ways to create energy and use it more efficiently. Imagine a day sometime in the future where energy is clean, quiet, and cheap to use. Several sources, such as the Sun and wind, hold that kind of promise.

Screaming for coffee
If you yelled for eight years, seven months, and six days, you would produce enough sound energy to heat one cup of coffee.

Tall turbine
Wind turbines keep getting bigger. As of 2010, the world's largest was in Germany, and had a blade span of 413 feet (126 m)—more than one and one-third football fields.

A window to inefficiency
A tiny crack just one sixteenth of an inch (1.6 mm) around a window frame can let in as much cold air as leaving the window open 3 inches (7.6 cm).

Racing with the Sun
Solar-powered race cars, such as the three-wheeled Nuna 5, can reach top speeds of around 93 miles (150 km) per hour. Not bad for a fully solar-powered vehicle!

Drip, drop, waste
A hot water faucet leaking just one drop per second adds up to 165 gallons (625 l) in a month. That is more water than most people use in two weeks.

Cooking with solar
British astronomer John Herschel traveled to Africa in the 1830s. On the expedition, he used a solar collector box to cook his meals.

Cold, hard facts
In the US, home refrigerators use the equivalent of the full output of 25 large power plants each year. Each time the refrigerator door is opened, as much as 30 percent of the cold air escapes.

It's Your Turn!

Choose one renewable energy source, such as solar, wind, or biofuels. Now, come up with a Top Facts list for that source. Try answering questions such as:

1 What advantages does the energy source have?

2 What are the disadvantages?

3 Can it be used anywhere in the world?

4 Is it widely used? If not, what would it take for it to become widely used?

5 Is it affordable to most people?

Make a poster
Collect your facts together and make them into a poster that promotes your energy source as a solution to energy problems. Try to include several photos that represent that form of energy.

Glossary

biofuels
(BY-oh-fyoolz)
Fuels that come from renewable, living sources, such as plants.

bioreactor
(by-oh-ree-AK-tur)
A machine that uses waste as a fuel source.

coal power
(KOHL POW-ur)
Power created by burning coal dug from the ground.

decompose
(dee-kum-POHZ)
To decay or break down.

fossil fuel
(FAH-sul FYOOL)
Any fuel, such as coal, petroleum, and natural gas, formed from fossilized remains of prehistoric plants and animals.

gas (GAS)
Another term for natural gas, as well as a shortened version of the word gasoline.

generator
(JEH-nuh-ray-tur)
A motor used in reverse to create electricity.

geothermal energy
(jee-oh-THUR-mul EH-ner-jee)
Power created by capturing the steam of naturally heated groundwater.

hydroelectric power
(hy-droh-ih-LEK-trik POW-ur)
Power created by flowing water turning turbines.

methane gas
(MEH-thayn GAS)
A naturally occurring, colorless, odorless gas that is produced by decomposition.

nacelle (nuh-SEL)
The structure on top of a wind turbine tower that holds the rotor shaft, gearbox, and generator.

nuclear energy
(NOO-klee-ur EH-nur-jee)
Energy created by harnessing atomic reactions.

open cut mine
(OH-pun KUT MYN)
A mine formed by making a huge pit cut into the ground. The minerals are removed and the hole remains.

peat (PEET)
Partly decayed vegetation.

petroleum
(peh-TROH-lee-um)
A liquid found in the ground formed from fossilized remains of ancient plants and animals. It is burned for fuel.

porous (POR-us)
Full of holes, letting through water and other liquids.

solar cells (SOH-lur SELZ)
Electronic circuits that capture sunlight using silicon crystals and generate electricity.

solar energy
(SOH-lur EH-nur-jee)
Energy created by the Sun.

tidal energy
(TY-dul EH-nur-jee)
Energy created by capturing the movement of water caused by tides.

turbine (TUR-byn)
A kind of engine turned by a moving fluid or air that produces electricity.

wind energy
(WIND EH-nur-jee)
Energy created by capturing the movement of air to turn a turbine.

Index

Websites

Due to the changing nature of Internet links, PowerKids Press has developed an online list of websites related to the subject of this book. This site is updated regularly. Please use this link to access the list:
www.powerkidslinks.com/disc/energy/

Energy Sources

Nature provides many forms of energy that people use every day in many ways. Energy powers our homes and vehicles, heats our water, and helps us do our work. There are two kinds of energy sources: renewable and non-renewable. Renewable sources, such as energy from the wind, Sun, and sea, are replenished by nature when they are used. Non-renewable sources, such as oil, gas, and coal, are not naturally replenished as fast as we use them. Once they are used, they are gone for thousands of years.

Where energy comes from

Fossil fuels, such as coal, petroleum (oil), and natural gas, are taken from the ground. Energy also comes from the Sun, and the movement of water and wind.

Oil and gas
These are found together in pockets in Earth's crust.

Coal
This is dug from the ground and burned to release its energy.

Nuclear energy
Nuclear power plants use radioactive decay of uranium atoms to release their energy.

Geothermal energy
This is created by capturing the steam of naturally heated groundwater.

Contents